WALKING WITH DINOSAURS

Photo Journal

THE JOURNEY BEGINS...

Imagine yourself travelling back through time, so far back that the entire history of humanity seems to have lasted barely a second. You're heading for a world that's very different from the one you know, an Earth where there are no countries and no people – just a humongous lump of land in the middle of a vast sea, ruled over by animals unlike any we might see in our own time.

It's time to go walking with the **dinosaurs**...

DINOSAUR DAWN

Open your eyes.

You're here. It's now. The Triassic Period, 220 million years in the past.

The first thing that hits you is the heat. The sun's beating down and you can feel it baking your skin and cracking your lips. As you move forwards, through clouds of lacewings and damselflies, through thick ferns and scrubland, already you are desperate for water.

Then you see them. The creatures…

Grazing at sunset

They don't stop eating!

They're everywhere... dozens of bulky, great **Placerias**, grubbing about for food, tearing up plants with their horns and swallowing them down, roots and all. Small, fat hatchlings, their horns not yet fully formed, dart about the landscape, finding roots and shoots to satisfy their growing appetites.

The Placerias eat only plants. I guess I'm safe. For now...

You duck back into the spindly trees. It's eerily calm as you walk along, uncomfortable in the baking midday heat.

Suddenly, a loud squawk carries through the dry air, making you jump. You look up to find a small, bird-like reptile, a **Peteinosaurus**, perched on a branch. It has just caught a lacewing, and as you watch, it devours the insect's body in just a few crunchy bites.

Peteinosaurus

Lacewing

FOREST ENCOUNTER

Suddenly, an enormous crashing from the forest sends the little Peteinosaurus clattering from the tree. Two **Plateosaurus** are lumbering through the vegetation, their oval heads bobbing about on their long necks. One rears up almost three metres above me to reach the greenery at the top of the trees. If I hang around here, I might be trampled into the ground...

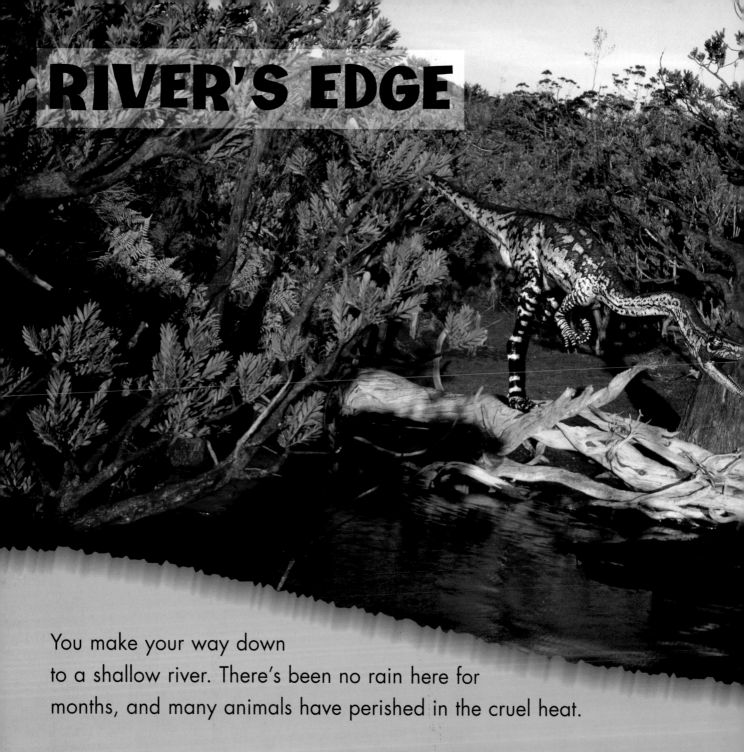

RIVER'S EDGE

You make your way down
to a shallow river. There's been no rain here for
months, and many animals have perished in the cruel heat.

Down by the water's edge, a pack of **Coelophysis** – quite small and
skinny, but very ferocious dinosaurs – are squabbling over who will get
the prime meat from a dying **Postosuchus**.

The crocodile-like reptile snaps its jaws at the Coelophysis, warning them
away. But it has been badly injured in a fight with a Plateosaurus, and
cannot survive much longer. The Coelophysis dart about the fallen reptile,
picking at its skin.

Soon the rains will come, bringing new life to the dying land. But it is too late for this Postosuchus. I close my eyes and turn away.

It's time to move forward to another dinosaur age....

Postosuchus

GIANT MOTHER

It's now 155 million years ago, during the Jurassic Period. The world is wetter now, and many of the old desert landscapes have become green with new plant-life.

I'm staring at the incredible sight of a **Diplodocus** mother in the morning sunlight.

She's so huge I can barely believe it. Her body's the size of two elephants, but with her snaking tail and huge, swaying neck, she must be well over thirty metres in length. That's as long as my local swimming pool!

This mother has just laid over a hundred eggs, each the size of a football, into large, circular holes. The babies will hatch underground before struggling to the surface. There, they must escape hungry meat-eaters like **Ornitholestes** by running into the dense cover of the forest.

Then, these baby dinosaurs will begin a life of endless eating. After just one year, each baby will weigh over a tonne.

Watch out – Ornitholestes is about!

FOLLOW
THE HERD...

When they are grown up, the Diplodocus can each weigh up to fifteen tonnes. The ground trembles beneath you as they crash through the fringes of the forest, tearing at the highest clumps of leaves with their clumsy, peg-like teeth. Diplodocus move in herds of about thirty. As you watch, each giant dinosaur reaches out its tail to touch others, making sure they're close by. Their tails are like giant snakes, twisting through the air, allowing the dinosaurs to keep in touch without interrupting their endless eating.

Look! This little creature is called **Anurognathus**. It settles down on the back of a Diplodocus, and lives there all its life.
That's what I call having a <u>real</u> mobile home!

And I thought it was only **humans** who weren't supposed to speak with their mouths full!

Gradually, the thundering footsteps of the Diplodocus herd grow fainter, as the giants plod onwards to new grazing lands.

ALLOSAURUS ATTACK!

Moving into the forest, you find yourself splashing through shallow water in a valley. It's warm. You're tired. You sit down and watch as two young Diplodocus in the distance eat ferns from the canyon walls. You begin to fall asleep – then you hear something growl...

It's an
Allosaurus –
big, savage and
deadly. Its beady
eyes are staring
at you from under
blood-red brows
as it sniffs the air.
An Allosaurus
would never attack
a fully grown
Diplodocus for fear
of being crushed –
but you'd make a
far easier meal...

Maybe I should stop snapping
and start running!

It stalks towards you on its powerful hind legs, its
smaller forearms twitching as it gets nearer. You can
see its muscles rippling under the tough, scaly skin...
But then a baby Diplodocus appears from the side of
the canyon – and falls straight into the slavering
carnivore's path. Before you can react, the Allosaurus
has grabbed the baby with its teeth and smashed it into
the ground.

There's nothing you can do to save it. You have to get
away before this killer finishes feeding and comes
after you again.

But then another Allosaurus lumbers into view...

SHOWDOWN!

The Allosaurus sees you and hisses, tramping forwards, pointed teeth glinting in the sunlight. You sprint as fast as you can, but it's no good. You can hear it gaining on you, its footsteps getting louder and faster, like the beating of your heart.

Then, suddenly, something pushes its way out through the trees right in front of you – a **Stegosaurus**. It's a plant-eater, but still deadly – its tail packs four spikes, each a metre long, so it can easily defend itself. And you've surprised it...

You slip on some wet mud as you dive out of the way. The huge herbivore's tail whistles over your head and smashes into a tree.

Then the Stegosaurus realises that the Allosaurus is approaching. It turns sideways to show off the armoured plates that bristle down its back, and flexes its tail menacingly. The Allosaurus looks first at you, then at the Stegosaurus… then slowly backs away. You can see the hunger in its eyes – but you're not worth battling for. It will look to feed elsewhere.

The Stegosaurus shuffles over to the stream to drink, apparently forgetting that you're there. Softly, slowly, you move away yourself, into the undergrowth.

Stegosaurus – vegetarian with attitude!

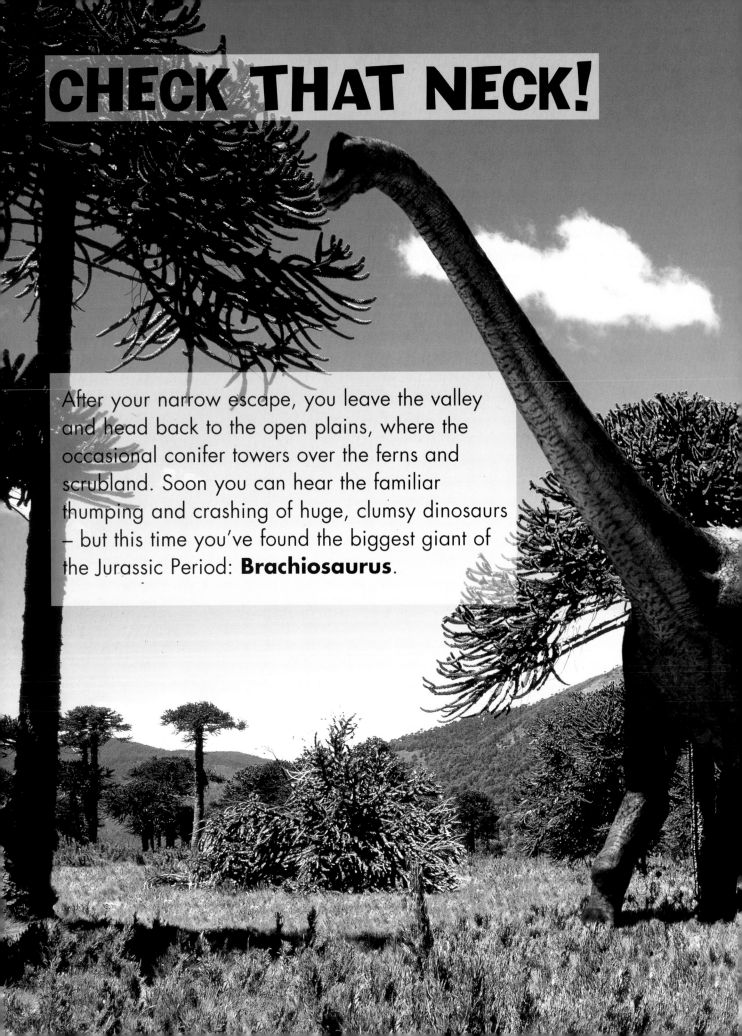

CHECK THAT NECK!

After your narrow escape, you leave the valley and head back to the open plains, where the occasional conifer towers over the ferns and scrubland. Soon you can hear the familiar thumping and crashing of huge, clumsy dinosaurs – but this time you've found the biggest giant of the Jurassic Period: **Brachiosaurus**.

There are two of them, so massive they dwarf even Diplodocus. Each of them weighs around seventy tonnes. Both Brachiosaurus are eating from the trees, and you wonder how there can be enough food to go round for all these giants. But while the Diplodocus eat plants at all heights, Brachiosaurus tend to feed on the treetops – and unlike Diplodocus, they have sharp teeth to cut through the leaves and cones, stripping the trees bare before lumbering on to their next meal.

It's an incredible sight, but I think I should move on to another time. The ferns that grow on these plains will tempt the young, hungry Diplodocus out from the forest – and wherever they go, the ever-watchful Allosaurus will follow, waiting for the kill...

A TRIP TO THE SEA

It's now 150,000,000 BC...

You've travelled forward through time some five million years. Now you're standing by the sea in the Cretaceous Period, on a warm island. Ahead of you, basking in the sun on a rock, is something that looks like a cross between a seal and the Loch Ness Monster – a creature called Cryptoclidus.

As you walk forward to get a closer look, the Cryptoclidus slithers into the sea. You dive in yourself and follow it.

Cryptoclidus uses its four large flippers to push itself through the water. It heads down to the seabed and pushes its head deep into the pale sand.

Wait a minute – what's it doing? Is it looking for food? No, hang on – it's swallowing stones!

Cryptoclidus's flippers move in patterns like figures-of-eight!

"That ammonite looks interesting!"

The stones stay in Cryptoclidus's gut, weighing the creature down so it can stay underwater longer.

Now it begins to feed, its long neck snaking about to catch fish. But there are other creatures in these warm waters to attract your attention…

SPEEDY SWIMMERS

Something big rushes past you in the water, startling you. It's an **Ophthalmosaurus**, about five metres long and the fastest thing in the sea — it just shot past you at fifty kilometres per hour. Unlike Cryptoclidus, Ophthalmosaurus uses its flippers for steering — its tail speeds it through the water.

You swim along further under the water, until you come to a vast cavern. Sunlight streams in through holes in the rock above, and you watch as masses of Ophthalmosaurus dart about looking for food. Their large eyes are sensitive to changes in light, and this helps to make them good hunters.

But another hunter lurks in the seas around this island. Its name is **Liopleurodon**, and it's the giant king of the ancient oceans, around twenty metres long. Its mouth is festooned with lethal teeth, and its sense of smell is horribly accurate… Liopleurodon is a threat to anything that lives in these waters – including you!

An undersea kingdom

Lurking Liopleurodon…

THE SCAVENGERS

Back on dry land, your troubles are hardly over. Soon you spot a nasty-looking dinosaur about seven metres long, tugging at some stubborn strands of meat that used to be a turtle. This is **Eustreptospondylus**, and the islands in this area are its home. There is not always enough food to go round, so this dinosaur will eat more or less anything it can get its fearsome teeth into. You duck out of sight, pressing your body against the hot sand, peeping to see what will happen next, scarcely daring to breathe…

Oh no – another evil-looking Eustreptospondylus is approaching, checking to see if there's food going spare. The first one growls a warning… Are they going to fight?

No… the newcomer backs down and stalks off to scavenge elsewhere.

Tasty turtle!

Eustreptospondylus knows only its terrible hunger. Like all other meat-eating dinosaurs, it is desperate to kill and feast on whatever victims it can find.

PTEROSAUR BEACH...

You move forward through time again, and find yourself on a rocky outcrop of land by the sea 145 million years ago. The skies seem alive as pterosaurs – flying reptiles – soar through the air above you. These ones are called **Tapejara**, and they're here to mate. On the ground, the males bustle about for the best positions to attract the circling females. Their heads are remarkable – you can't help but stare at the big red sails of skin and bone rising up from their beaks.

The noise is deafening – not just the roaring of the sea, but the squawking and the clacking of huge beaks as the males squabble with each other for the best spot.

Suddenly, I see another pterosaur soaring past. It's an Ornithocheirus, and it's absolutely **huge** – its wings are the length of a double-decker bus!

I think I'll see where it's going...

Who will be top Tapejara?

HIGH-FLYER

The **Ornithocheirus** takes off from the outcrop, his huge leathery wings flapping to lift his bulk from the ground. He will fly for thousands of kilometres to reach the place where he was born – then, like Tapejara, he will be forced to compete with other, younger Ornithocheirus for a mate.

He stops on his journey when a tropical storm breaks. The downpour of water prevents him from flying, and so he shelters under an overhang of shady rock on the beach until the storm passes. He spends the time picking at blood-sucking parasites with his long beak. When the storm passes, he will fish for food in the water, then continue on his incredible voyage.

I think I'll move on too!

A nit-picking pterosaur!

HUNTED!

Further along the beach, you come across a herd of **Iguanodon**. These creatures are living proof of how dinosaur design has improved over millions of years: you notice that they actually chew their food instead of swallowing it whole, to digest it faster. This is good news for the Iguanodon, which is basically a three-tonne eating machine!

The herd seems suddenly nervous... There's danger here, in the form of a **Utahraptor**. This deadly predator will use its huge claws and sharp teeth to tear into its prey until the poor animal bleeds to death!

The worried herd moves along the beach, while the Utahraptor watches out for any stragglers that might make an easy kill. Then another, quite extraordinary, animal grabs your attention...

Hungry Utahraptor...

...Frightened Iguanodon!

LONE WANDERER

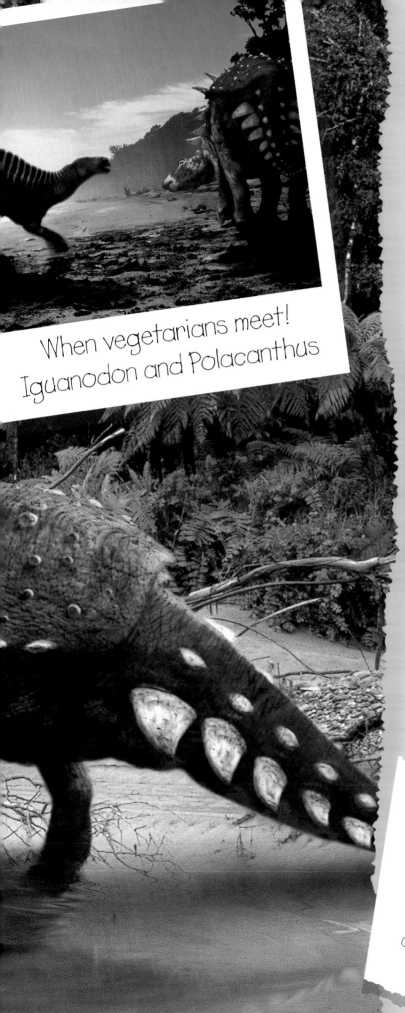

When vegetarians meet!
Iguanodon and Polacanthus

A curious bundle of lethal-looking spikes and armour lifts its head from a patch of shrubland. But this animal is no immediate threat. It's a **Polacanthus**, and eats only plants. It's probably hanging around with the Iguanodon herd because they will lead it to plenty of food.

It paddles through the water to reach another clump of plants, pulling at them with its narrow beak. Unlike the Iguanodon, Polacanthus can't chew its food – the vegetation ferments in its stomach instead.

An Iguanodon rushes past the Polacanthus, hooting in panic because the Utahraptor is about. The Polacanthus arches its armoured back and calls out a warning to the predator.

The sound is chilling. It's strange – I suppose the dinosaur world is just the same as a giant safari park – the animals eat and sleep and fight and kill... and there's no one at all to get in their way...

COLD JOURNEY

You drift forwards in time to 105,900,000 BC, and you're in a cold, dark forest. This is the South Pole, but long before it became a frozen wilderness of ice. There's sunshine and daylight for half the year, and nothing but chilly darkness for the other half.

The sun is beginning to set now. You hear an eerie cry floating through the twilight as a herd of **Muttaburrasaurus** comes into view. These huge herbivores have spent the summer grazing in the polar forests. Now they must migrate to warmer lands to find more food before they freeze.

The call is heard...

...by the herd!

But lurking in the shadows, following the herd and waiting for its moment to kill, is a **dwarf allosaur** – a distant relative of the Allosaurus you met earlier.

Just one look at its sharp teeth is enough to make you leave this time to a point almost 40 million years later...

This dwarf allosaur isn't so small!

T. REX TERROR!

You arrive in a forest clearing during the Late Cretaceous Period. In front of you is a large mound of steaming earth. An awful smell hangs in the air. There are masses of volcanoes erupting at this time in history, and the air is being poisoned as a result. The dinosaurs' world is under threat.

Crossing to the edge of the clearing, you see a huge dinosaur sniffing for food down by a stream. A shiver runs through you at the sight of its powerful legs and tiny arms.

A living nightmare...

Then you hear a low growl behind you. You spin round to find another of the giant creatures watching you.

Nothing you've seen on your travels can prepare you for the sight of **Tyrannosaurus rex**, the Tyrant Reptile King, lumbering towards you. The mound of earth is its nest, and this T. rex thinks you're trying to steal its eggs. It towers above you, bares its colossal teeth and roars...

FACE-OFF!

This Torosaurus baby couldn't escape in time...

The scariest carnivore that ever lived!

The T. rex isn't as fast on its feet as you imagined it would be. Sprinting away, imagining the monster's banana-sized teeth lifting you up and snapping you in two, you reach another clearing – and an unexpected ally. **Torosaurus**, a three-horned herbivore, is grazing a little way from its herd. It looks up and bellows at the sight of T. rex crashing through the forest behind you.

You circle round behind the Torosaurus as the T. rex roars again. The ten-tonne herbivore is no easy catch, and it makes a false charge at the roaring dinosaur, warning it to keep away. The T. rex lowers its head and bares its teeth again, shifting its bulk from foot to foot as it sizes up the Torosaurus. But then it turns and heads back the way it came.

Of course – the T. rex was a female! She wanted me away from her nest, and now that I've gone she's going back to watch over it again.

BIG HEADS!

It must be the mating season for Torosaurus. Just look at the huge, colourful crest on this male! Its size and brightness show how healthy and strong it is – I wouldn't want to tangle with this one!

Torosaurus had the largest head of any land animal!

Sometimes the males challenge each other, waving their massive heads about, each trying to prove it is the stronger. If neither backs down, they may lock horns and push against each other to settle the dispute.

It's the dinosaur equivalent of sumo wrestling!

The herd wanders across the hardened lava plains that have destroyed the vegetation here. Food is less plentiful by this time, and the dinosaurs must keep on the move.

Heavy traffic!

A MOMENT'S PEACE

You trail the Torosaurus herd for a while, then spy a large lake. You head off to drink from it, and notice a group of quite curious-looking duck-billed dinosaurs. These are **Anatotitan**, and they feed in small groups on the rich plantlife that grows down by the water.

Nice spot for an Anatotitan picnic!

They'd better watch out. Crocodiles that are as long as a bus lurk in these rivers, and can eat a young Anatotitan as easily as I can eat a sandwich!

After all your adventures, it's a relief to spend some time relaxing with the gentle Anatotitan. But then an awful thought strikes you...

METEOR!

It's 65,219,977 BC, a date with so many numbers and so long ago it seems almost meaningless. But something is coming. Something due to arrive any time now. A huge rock travelling through space, a **meteor**, is approaching the Earth at 240,000 kilometres per hour. It's going to crash into the ground so fast and so hard that 400,000,000,000,000 tonnes of rock, dust and ash are going to be thrown up into the sky, blocking out the sun. The temperature will drop to well below freezing, and acid rain will fall relentlessly.

What will become of the dinosaurs?

The dinosaurs ruled the world for 165 million years, but they died out around this time – along with two-thirds of all life on Earth. Scientists think that the impact of the meteor was responsible.

Few things could survive such a terrible natural disaster – not even a seasoned time-traveller like you. As the sun starts to set, like a fat, red orange in the sky, you leave behind the savage splendour of the prehistoric world and return home.

SCRAPBOOK

It's not just the memories of your prehistoric holiday you'll take back with you... here are pictures of some of the creatures you encountered on your travels! Check back through your photo journal and see if you can label each one correctly!

...e dinosaurs.
...ey were the mightiest
...eatures ever to walk the Earth...

...d with new dinosaur fossils being
...ound all the time, they will never be
...orgotten.

How to say the names of the creatures in this book...

PLACERIAS:	PLAH-sare-EE-ass
PETEINOSAURUS:	puh-TAIN-uh-SAW-rus
PLATEOSAURUS:	PLAY-tee-uh-SAW-rus
COELOPHYSIS:	SEE-luh-FYE-sis
POSTOSUCHUS:	POST-o-SUSH-us
DIPLODOCUS:	di-PLOH-duh-kus
ORNITHOLESTES:	OR-ni-thuh-LES-teez
ANUROGNATHUS:	Ah-NYUR-oh-NAYTH-us
ALLOSAURUS:	AL-uh-SAW-rus
STEGOSAURUS:	STEG-uh-SAW-rus
BRACHIOSAURUS:	BRACK-ee-uh-SAW-rus
CRYPTOCLIDUS:	CRIP-tuh-CLEE-dus
OPHTHALMOSAURUS:	op-THAL-mo-SAW-rus
LIOPLEURODON:	LYE-oh-PLUR-oh-don
EUSTREPTOSPONDYLUS:	yoo-STREP-toh-spon-DIL-us
TAPEJARA:	tap-eh-YAR-ah
ORNITHOCHEIRUS:	or-NITH-oh-KYR-us
IGUANODON:	i-GWAN-uh-don
UTAHRAPTOR:	YOO-tah-RAP-tor
POLACANTHUS:	POH-luh-KAN-thus
MUTTABURRASAURUS:	MUT-uh-BUR-uh-SAW-rus
TYRANNOSAURUS REX:	tye-RAN-uh-SAW-rus RECKS
TOROSAURUS:	TOR-uh-SAW-rus
ANATOTITAN:	uh-NAT-uh-TYE-tan

Cryptoclidus

Utahraptor

Allosaurus

Published by BBC Worldwide Ltd, Woodlands,
80 Wood Lane, London W12 OTT
First published 2000
Text by Stephen Cole & design by Tony Fleetwood,
copyright © BBC Worldwide Ltd 1999
Scientific adviser to BBC Worldwide: Dr Joanna Wright, University of Colorado
BBC commissioned photographs © BBC Worldwide Ltd 1999
Walking with Dinosaurs logo © BBC 1998
Licensed by BBC Worldwide Ltd
Walking with Dinosaurs word mark and logo are trademarks of the British Broadcasting Corporation.
Printed and bound by Tien Wah Press (Pte) Ltd Singapore